Mansions in Your Memory

Mansions in Your Memory

• • •

Jack McCall

Copyright © 2016 Jack McCall
All rights reserved.

ISBN 13: 9781533482075
ISBN-10: 1533482071
Library of Congress Control Number: 2016908764
CreateSpace Independent Publishing Platform
North Charleston, South Carolina

Contents

Introduction · vii

Chapter 1	Walk with Me: Part 1 · · · · · · · · · · · · · · · · ·	1
Chapter 2	Walk with Me: Part 2 · · · · · · · · · · · · · · · · ·	5
Chapter 3	Walk with Me: Part 3 · · · · · · · · · · · · · · · · ·	9
Chapter 4	Snowfall in the Brim Hollow · · · · · · · · ·	13
Chapter 5	Surprise in the Brim Hollow · · · · · · · · · ·	17
Chapter 6	"Old Hurry" ·	21
Chapter 7	Characters ·	25
Chapter 8	Harvest Sounds · · · · · · · · · · · · · · · · · ·	31
Chapter 9	Tobacco Rows ·	37
Chapter 10	Plowing Tobacco · · · · · · · · · · · · · · · · · ·	41
Chapter 11	Dropping Sticks · · · · · · · · · · · · · · · · · · ·	45
Chapter 12	Memories of My Dad · · · · · · · · · · · · · · · ·	51
Chapter 13	Boyhood Memories of Dew Roy Neal · · ·	57
Chapter 14	A Good Humor ·	63
Chapter 15	Gravel Roads ·	69
Chapter 16	Pope's Hill ·	75
Chapter 17	The Smell of Skunks · · · · · · · · · · · · · · · ·	81
Chapter 18	The Rifleman ·	85
Chapter 19	A Visit with an Old Friend · · · · · · · · · · · ·	91

Introduction

• • •

OF THE MANY GIFTS I received from my parents, two of the best came from my mother in the forms of a vivid imagination and an exceptional memory. Thanks to an extended, loving family, the lion's share of my memories is a good one. My parents, brothers, sister, grandfathers, grandmothers, uncles, aunts, cousins, and neighbors all played a part in creating a past to which I often return without pause. The best of my memories I find to be galvanizing.

In telling my stories over the years, I have found my best work is accomplished by reminding others of their own stories. Everyone has a story.

I have come to call recalling your best memories "drawing on the equity in your life." An old boy from North Carolina, a few years back, suggested it be called, "building mansions in your memory." He went on to say, "You can always go back and visit the mansions."

I think he was correct.

In the following pages, I invite you to visit a few of my mansions. Some may take the strangest forms—a water bucket, a snowfall, a personality, a hallowed spot. Hopefully, some will take you back to mansions of your own.

CHAPTER 1

Walk with Me: Part 1

• • •

My maternal grandfather, Will Herod Brim, known to most of his friends and family in the Riddleton Community as "John Reuben," died on November 12, 1963. In the fifty-plus years he's been gone, I have visited the Brim Hollow, where he spent most of his life, more times than I could count.

I still go there often, mostly in my mind. Today, I invite you to walk with me as I take you into the house that still holds some of my best childhood memories.

We are standing at the side of the house right now. (In the almost thirteen years I knew my grandfather, I never entered his house through the front door).

A big, heavy wooden door built with solid four- and six-inch boards greets us. At the foot of the door lies a rough-hewn rock step that couldn't be lifted by half a dozen men. To the left of the step stands two menacing blocks of wood. They are oddly shaped and fully three feet tall. I never knew their purpose.

Between the left-hand end of the step and the blocks of wood can be found a flat piece of metal. It is about eighteen inches long, an inch and a half wide, and as thin as the blade on a good butcher's knife. I tell you this because it is one of two keys to opening the door.

Over many years the hinges had weakened, causing the old heavy door to drag badly. In time, deep grooves had been cut into the floor inside in the shape of a quarter circle. The dragging door had also caused the locking mechanism to fall out of line. To unlock the door, you had to slip the flat piece of metal under the door and, using it as a pry bar, raise the door until the lock lined up. Once in place, the bar had to be negotiated with your left foot while you managed the door key with your hand.

It all sounds quite complicated, but it was really very simple. Unless you knew the "combination," you could not get through that door. You might call it a security system of yesteryear.

We're in the house now and find ourselves in the utility room. Looking up, we can see the underside of the tin roof. The wall to our right is unfinished. The wall studs are fashioned of rough lumber and are fully two by four. Between those studs, at floor level, my grandfather has stacked old plow points and retired ax-heads. Behind the door hangs his favorite bucksaw. In the center of the wall, on a big nail, is where he hung his overcoat and Stetson at the end of the day. Other nails secured other things.

The other side of the room is the "catch-all" part of the house. The far-left corner features a large wardrobe made of a heavy cardboard-type material. From the ceiling a heavy wire hook secures mounds of plaited ropes fashioned from used hay-baling strings. Three one-gallon buckets sit on the floor, in the right-hand corner of the room. They are filled with rusted nuts and bolts, crooked and rusted nails, crooked steeples, pieces of broken hinges, and anything metal my grandfather might have picked up during the course of the day

I have to push the door open (it has a tendency to drag, also) as we enter the largest room in the house, the kitchen. As we step inside, a refrigerator stands backed up to the wall, immediately to our left. On the other side of the refrigerator stands my grandmother's pie safe. It is the kind that stands on legs and has the tin panels decorated with little holes in the doors. Those little holes let the air in and kept the flies out!

We are now looking at the big kitchen table, covered in red-and-white-checked oilcloth. My late mother remembered when her father built that table. The total cost was seventy-five cents. One end of the table rests against the wall under a big, wide window. I must share with you who sat at the head of that table for the meals I remember—and much more about this room filled with memories.

CHAPTER 2

Walk with Me: Part 2

● ● ●

We are now in the center of the kitchen. As we stand at the end of the table opposite the wall, I am presented with a scene all too familiar to me. In my earliest years, I remember sitting there atop two Sears & Roebucks catalogs in a straight-back chair.

It was I who sat at the head of the table. Like a king on his throne, I ruled my kingdom from there. My grandfather sat to my left. My grandmother sat to my right, with her back to the woodstove.

From my vantage point, I could survey my Brim Hollow universe. Across the long table and through the wide window, I could see the smokehouse straight ahead, the chicken house to the left, and the path that led to the outhouse between the two. The wide window, when opened, drew a cool breeze from beneath shade trees that stood sentry over the house and yard.

Outside the house, a shelf, about twelve inches wide, was attached to the base of the window. A wire screen ran from the top of the window to enclose the shelf, creating a boxlike effect. My grandmother would open the window and set out hot pies to cool on that shelf.

Just beyond the kitchen table, we see my grandmother's pride and joy—her woodstove. It is only a step away from the table. When I was a boy, the stove seemed monstrously large, deep, and very wide. We still have the stove today. It appears very small to me now. But not then!

On the left-hand side of the stove was attached a copper water reservoir. It provided a continuous supply of hot water all year round—rainwater, I might add—but it was used neither for drinking nor for cooking. My grandmother was a wizard when it came to cooking with a woodstove. It was her stove of choice eleven months out of the years. In July she reluctantly gave it up and used her electric stove—but only in July!

I especially remember my grandmother's "dog bread." It was made with course-ground cornmeal and side-meat drippings; it was a wonder. I can still smell the aroma as the oven door was opened. A boy I knew well was known to slip in and eat the crust off the dog bread from time to time.

Turning from the front of the woodstove to our right, we see the back wall of the kitchen. A door in the far right corner of the room leads to the screened back porch. To the left of the door stands the electric stove. It was one of those stoves that stood on four legs. The oven was on the right side, almost at eye level, and there were three heating units built in to the left of the oven. A cabinet stood to the left of the stove. It was one of those that contained a flour bin. You could turn a little crank and sift flour right onto the work area.

The stovetop and countertop served as the area where my grandmother plucked her frying chickens. Sometimes when I return to the old kitchen in my mind, I get an unpleasant whiff of scalded chicken feathers.

I spent very little time in the kitchen when my grandmother was plucking chickens. I did, however, from time to time, get a glimpse of a big pan piled high with gray chicken innards. I never looked for long!

We are at the back door of the kitchen now. As I swing it open, we are met with one of the dominant features of the back porch: the water bucket. It is white with red trim. The ever-present dipper is silver aluminum. The bucket is suspended from the ceiling with a long piece of no. 9 wire, with hooks in each end. The water in that bucket, hand-drawn from a well, was almost as sweet as spring water and almost as cold all year round.

Oops! I'll have to leave you at the water bucket. If you have ever sipped water out of a dipper from a water bucket, take a few moments to remember how cool and refreshing it tasted.

I'll meet you on the back porch in the next chapter.

CHAPTER 3

Walk with Me: Part 3

● ● ●

In the last chapter, I left you on the back porch. Actually it was not a porch at all, but that's what we called it. It was a small, narrow room about four feet wide and as long as the kitchen. The outside wall was boxed up about four feet high. A screen ran from the top of the wall to the ceiling.

As we step out on the porch, we have a full view through the screen door of the backyard and, beyond, my grandmother's garden. The right-hand side of the garden was devoted to growing things to eat. The left side was reserved for my grandmother's flower garden.

In the springtime the sight of her flowers was breathtaking. In the early spring, buttercups were everywhere. Some were big and country-egg-yolk yellow, and some were ghostly white. There was one she called "butter 'n' eggs" and a dainty white one she called "wedding bells." The varieties and colors seemed endless. Later in the spring came the iris. You would never have seen the likes of her iris. They grew in families of colors—: deepest purples, canary yellows, sky blues, lavenders, soft peaches, purple, white…the list could go on.

The sight of my grandmother's flowers always put me in a good humor. Whenever I visit that flower garden in my mind, I can't help but smile.

Back on the porch, turning to our left, we see the back wall of the porch covered with shelves. Empty glass jars, glass bottles, vases, and odd and ends fill the shelves (things that won't freeze in winter). About halfway down the outside wall, a water faucet rests eighteen inches above the floor. It brings water through a galvanized pipe from the rain barrel. You can't miss the rain barrel as you look through the porch screen.

My late mother told of the day they set that rain barrel in its place. She was just a little girl then. Two logs on each side fashioned a square platform on which the rain barrel rested. The floor underneath the barrel was built with red cedar boards (at my grandfather's insistence). The boards are still there and so is the barrel. My mother would have been ninety-seven this year.

Please note that over the years, holes in the walls of the water tank have been mended with small bolts and nuts, washers, and squares of red tire inner tubing.

Rainwater was used for washing and watering chickens. Humans should not drink rainwater—at least, that is what I was told. However, I did try it a few times. Rainwater has a hard taste to it. But I stopped drinking it when I found out "red wigglers" lived in the rain barrel.

Let's step outside for a moment. That's OK; just let the screen door close itself. It's spring-loaded, you know. There's no sound as sweet as the slamming of a screen door. That sound brings back so many memories for me. It recalls a time when real people lived real lives in real houses.

Sometimes when the screen door didn't close fast enough to suit him, my grandfather would yell, "Shut that screen door! You're lettin' all the flies out!"

Looking to your left around the rain barrel, you will note that the backyard slopes rather steeply. That mound with the ceiling made of big, flat rocks is the milk house. It has rock walls on the inside. Come closer, and I'll show you the steps that take you down inside. My grandmother used to cool the cow's milk in that pool of water at the bottom.

Be careful as we walk around the backyard. Touch-me-nots and four-o'clocks grow among those rocks sticking up out of the ground. (Those are flowers, in case you don't know). And one other thing. See that little tree leaning toward the house? A tree frog once lived in that very tree. He could sing quite a song on a summer's night.

Thanks for taking the time to walk with me. I hope I have inspired you to take a walk of your own.

CHAPTER 4

Snowfall in the Brim Hollow

• • •

ONE OF MY FAVORITE SETTINGS in the world is the Brim Hollow as it lies silently under a blanket of newly fallen snow. Sometimes when the weather seems most unforgiving, I will make the trek to this place I have known so well. Alone in a quiet, undisturbed winter wonderland, I find a peace and deep satisfaction that comes to me in no other place.

There I feel a oneness with the beauty that only God could create. As I take in all the sights and sounds, the word "pristine" comes to my mind.

There is great medicine in finding oneself completely alone, sometimes. It gives you time to clear your head and think—and listen—and hopefully hear.

A heavy blanket of snow has a way of muffling noise of any kind. In a strange way, the very silence has a sound of its own. But you have to listen carefully. When you do, you begin to hear that which you would ordinarily miss.

It's been a while since I ventured into the Brim Hollow on a snowy day.

The last time I was there, my Toyota pickup delivered me up the road to a scene I have witnessed a thousand times. The old homeplace, flanked by the chicken house and the remains of the old smokehouse, stood gray and forlorn against the winter's white.

I left the truck, laid my deer rifle on my shoulder, and headed up the hollow. After only a few steps, I stopped to take in the beauty surrounding me. The trees were heavy with snow as they stood gray, naked of their leaves in the winter landscape. I thought of the words of Robert Frost: "The woods are lovely, dark and deep…"

As I continued my walk, the sound of the snow crunching under my boots made me smile. The hollow road took me down into a rock creek bed called "the narrow place" and on past the yard of what we have always called "the little house." It is fallen now, unattended for too many winters.

Further up the hollow road, I walked on layers of brown leaves frozen tightly against the ground. They made a crackling sound as they broke beneath me.

As I reached the head of the Brim Hollow, I observed the log barn and the old feed barn. Their tired frames are now stooping to the passing of the years. I peered inside their empty stables, unvisited by cattle and sheep and mules for over three-quarters of a century. I tried to envision the days when these old friends were bustling with activity—when each stable was in use, when the crib was filled with corn, and the loft was piled high with hay.

As I looked outside, I saw the gray forms of rock fences. Like old weathered tentacles, they reached out in odd directions through the blanket of snow. I stopped beside the rock wall of an old springhouse.

Brushing the snow off a flat rock, I sat down and listened. On one of the ridges, the wind, stirring through the trees, made a sound much like the roar of a distant waterfall. High on a hill, I heard the unmistakable sound of a woodpecker driving his chisel beak into a hardwood. Down the hollow I heard a singular, familiar birdcall.

Then I heard the quiet—the sound of nothing. If you have ever been there, you know of what I speak.

I watched my frosty breath rise in front of my face. And I reveled in the joy of my solitude.

The whistle of a deer broke the silence. I slumped down behind the rock wall so I would not be discovered. I watched as six does passed unhurriedly below a ridge in single file. I was pleased with myself because my presence was undiscovered.

As I headed out of the hollow, I heard a deep "hoot hoot" up to my left. It could have easily been mistaken for a hoot owl, but the hoots were too far apart; I had heard that voice before. I think it was the call of a coyote. No matter—I was ready to leave him in his world.

I had found that for which I was seeking—a rested mind and a cleansed spirit. You can bet the next big snowfall will find me back in the Brim Hollow.

CHAPTER 5

Surprise in the Brim Hollow

• • •

I missed this year's first snowstorm. I spent most of that storm's days either trying to get out of Middle Tennessee or trying to get back. But when the second storm came, I was ready.

On the morning after the snow had fallen, I was on my way to the Brim Hollow. After leaving Bowman's Branch, I could have driven most of the way, but I chose to walk. Once I was well along the hollow road, I was surprised to find the branch running full but unhurried. You may have called it a creek, but my granny, Lena, always referred to it as "the branch."

The sounds of that branch—running cold, singing, laughing, sizzling, and whispering—would accompany me for my entire journey this winter's day. But it never broke the silence that I had come to love. It, instead, enhanced it. Strangely, the sounds of the rushing water became a part of the quiet.

A redbird greeted me as I drew closer to the hollow's entrance gate. He only lingered long enough to trumpet a welcome—he did so without uttering a note of song. His magnificent presence was sufficient. A male cardinal against a backdrop of winter's white sports a hue of unmatched red.

The only other vivid colors I would see this day were a redheaded woodpecker's beret as he hammered away on a decaying log barn and the greenest green moss on the shady side of an ancient rock fence. All the rest was wonderfully white and wintery.

As I walked along, I discovered the occasional signs of a big-footed coyote and, here and there, lightly traveled deer trails marked by the shape of hooves. All the while, the ever-present sounds of the branch kept me company, its waters cascading, pouring, and surging past.

By the time I reached the head of the hollow, I had made my decision. I would not climb higher and follow a ridge back toward the hollow's entrance, as I had done so many times before. The branch had cast a deliciously intoxicating spell on me. I was drawn to follow its path back out of Brim Hollow, allowing myself to be mesmerized by its laughing, singing currents.

As I made my leisurely retreat, I took the time to study in more detail the object of this day's delight: little pools that gave way to tiny waterfalls; places where the branch widened; where the water, a half inch deep, sizzled across a flat, rock floor; little eddies that released themselves over a maze of tangled tree roots, only to crackle down and stairstep the broken rocks; and narrows where the current rushed faster toward its ocean home.

Alone in the Brim Hollow with my only companions—the snow, the cold, and the music of the stream—I felt the strange and wonderful sensation of being really alive. Maybe you've known that feeling—when you feel a part of something much, much larger and grander than yourself, when your spirit soars, and you sense a thankfulness that cannot be expressed in words.

CHAPTER 6

"Old Hurry"

● ● ●

My late mother told me many stories of her growing up in the Brim Hollow. One of the most memorable involved a horse named "Old Hurry."

Herod Brim, her father, was a curious fellow. He was eccentric and somewhat distant as a father. I think my mother lived much of her life never quite sure of how he felt about her. He referred to her as "son" until she was almost seven years old. That fact alone should have given her reason to wonder.

I only knew him for my first twelve years. Personally, I think he adored her. But I was seeing through my eyes, not hers.

My mother loved to tell about Old Hurry. Before I finish the story, you will understand why.

It seems there was no shortage of horses and mules in the Brim Hollow in the 1920s and 1930s. There were riding horses, along with horses trained to pull the buggies and mules for doing the heavy work. As a little girl, my mother knew all their names. The horse she remembered best was Old Hurry.

Most of the horses and mules were kept "up close" in the big lot that surrounded the house and feed barns. Often, they rested under big trees just outside the yard.

"As a little girl, I was always suspect of Old Hurry," she told me. "He had a mean look in his eyes. When he was nearby, I never took my eyes off him."

One day, as she was walking to the barn, Old Hurry made his move.

"Suddenly I heard hoofbeats, and out of nowhere he came storming toward me, his teeth bared and his ears laid back," she said. "I ran for my life!"

Fortunately, my little skinny-legged mother made it to the safety of the barn. She later earned the nickname Killdeer (pronounced "kill-dee") because she had skinny legs and was fleet of foot.

When the danger had passed, she told her father of how Old Hurry had chased her that day. "Well, let's just see" was his reply.

So the two of them devised a plan to expose Old Hurry's mean streak.

As her father hid behind the smokehouse, he sent her on a walk to the barn right out in full view of Old Hurry. And sure enough, here he came; his ears laid back and his white teeth flashing!

"Papa came out from behind the smokehouse, hollering and throwing rocks, and Old Hurry ran for the hills." She beamed.

But that's not how the story ended.

"The next morning when I went out to play, Old Hurry was gone. I never saw him again. And I never asked what happened to him."

She speculated that Old Hurry was sent to the stock sale or traded, even though she was never sure. But two things she knew for certain: he was dealt with overnight, and he never chased her again.

My mother loved to tell that story. In it, she was shown how her father valued her. I have learned over the years that a child's greatest need is to feel valued. And when they are shown that someone considers them valuable, they remember it for a long, long time.

CHAPTER 7

Characters

• • •

On October 29, 2011, my mother passed away. I had plenty of time to prepare myself for the inevitable. We were with her as a family when she died. She went peacefully.

Both my mother and my father left their children with a priceless final gift: a good death. Neither one blinked in the face of death. Both faced their final hours with a calmness and assurance that one should expect of a child of God.

In days gone by, my mother told me how in her lifetime she had been present at the moment of death for four individuals. According to her experience, death was "really not that big of a deal." That's how she approached hers.

Growing old for her was a different subject. "Growing old," she often declared, "is no fun! At least it hasn't been for me! Don't let anyone kid you."

I will have to cut her a little slack on the subject of growing old. For the last ten or so years of her life, she was legally blind and forced to use a walker. And she watched as all but one of her best friends died one by one. She greatly missed her sight, and she greatly missed her friends.

But for the most part, she maintained a good attitude. My mother was one of those people with whom you love to be around. I miss her.

Lately I have been experiencing a kind of dull numbness. I can't quite put my finger on it. I've decided it is just something you have to push through after you have given up someone whom you loved deeply.

Speaking of losing someone, after my father died, someone at my mother's church expressed sympathy to my mother in "the loss of your husband."

"Loss?" my mother replied. "I haven't lost him. I know exactly where he is!"

My mother was a *character*. And she had every right to be. Her father was a *character*. I could, and I may, write a book about him.

His name was Will Herod Brim. To this day, stories still surface about the things he had said and done. One came out of Hartsville a few years ago.

It seems M. H. "Snukes" Duncan and his father were friends of my grandfather. (By the way, M. H. stood for Mort Herod.) Mr. Duncan and my grandfather were the only two men named Herod that I have ever known.

The story, as told by Snukes Duncan, goes this way. The two Mr. Duncans arrived in the Brim Hollow, intent on buying a bull my grandfather had for sale. My grandfather led them to the pound where the bull was kept. The potential buyers stepped through the pound gate to get a look at the bull.

As the bull walked by them, Snukes leaned toward his father and, speaking of the bull, said, "He's a little shy in the rear end, ain't he?"

Upon hearing what Snukes said, my grandfather barked, "Open the gate, and let him out! He's not for sale!"

Caught completely off guard, Snukes stammered, "I didn't mean I didn't like him, Mr. Brim! I was just saying…"

"Open the gate and let him out, I said!" snarled my grandfather. "He's not for sale!"

That ended the bull buying.

My grandfather grew up a Methodist. Before my mother was born, he often attended the Riddleton Baptist Church with my grandmother.

One Sunday, at the close of the service, the Sunday-school superintendent said, "Mr. Brim, please pray our closing prayer."

My grandfather, thinking he was the one being called upon, began to pray. He was about three or four words into his prayer, when he was interrupted by the superintendent saying, "I didn't mean *you*. I meant the other Mr. Brim." It was a mortally embarrassing moment for him.

Will Herod Brim "never set foot in the Baptist church again."

But he encouraged my mother to be a Baptist.

"You go with your mother," he told his daughter. "I want you to be a 'Bob-tist.' The Bob-tist believe 'once in and never out.'"

Of course, he was speaking of the principle, "once saved, always saved," or that which the Presbyterians refer to as "the security of the saints" or "the perseverance of the saints."

There is a line in a song titled, *Old Time Religion*, which goes like this: "It will *do* when I am dying."

It was good enough for my father…and my mother. And it's good enough for me.

CHAPTER 8

Harvest Sounds

● ● ●

I stopped by an old tobacco barn a few weeks back. Except for a trailer wagon from which I used to get a few bales of hay, the barn was empty.

It smelled like an empty tobacco barn. As I looked up through the tier poles devoid of hanging tobacco, I thought of how in a few weeks, if only for a day or two, the barn would come alive with the sounds of bustling activity as it was filled to the tin roof. It made me pause and consider the many sounds of a tobacco harvest.

The first sound of which I thought was the sound of my father sharpening the tobacco knives, and even the spikes, with a flat file. Whether we were chopping corn or tobacco, or beginning tobacco-cutting season, a familiar fixture was a big, flat file in my father's left hip pocket. That raspy sound of metal on metal is one of which I am well familiar.

Next I thought of the crashing sound of bundles of tobacco sticks being pitched on a wagon bed or truck bed. It is a loud crackling sound, much like a clap of thunder that comes too close. But there is really no other sound quite like it.

Then I thought of the unique popping sound made when the blade of a tobacco knife slices through a ripe tobacco stalk.

It is almost musical—the rhythmic "pop, pop, pop" as tobacco is laid down. Whether cut with a pull knife (drawknife) or a hatchet, the sound is much the same.

When the late Dr. Hugh Green's boys were old enough to do farmwork, he started a farming operation. Someone asked him why he, being a physician, started growing tobacco. He answered, "I'm not growing tobacco. I'm growing boys!"

My best childhood friend, Hugh Green Jr., and his brothers found themselves fully engaged in the business of tobacco growing. By the time the Green boys came along, the hatchet tobacco knife was being widely used, but it had not made its way to the Frank McCall farm. We still used the pull knife. It was not easily given up.

I remember three "pull" knives in particular that we used over the years. One was fashioned from a steel rod. The end of the rod had been beaten flat. Two rivets held the knife blade in place. The other end of the rod was bent at a ninety-degree angle in the opposite direction of the blade to form a handle. A wooden spool, about five inches long, had been slipped over the metal. The wooden handle was covered with black cloth tape. It was a sweet tobacco knife.

Another knife was made from a small ax handle. The curved handle fit your hand like a glove. You could cut tobacco all day without a glove and never get a blister. But my favorite tobacco knife had a straight, round wooden handle. The blade had been cut out of a Ford Model T fender. It was some kind of metal. That blade would hold an edge like the blade of a fine pocketknife.

Over the span of two or three years, Hugh Green Jr. and I had some serious debates over tobacco knives. He insisted the hatchet was superior. I, on the other hand, held out that the pull knife was far superior.

After all, what did he know? He was a doctor's son and a city boy. My father, on the other hand, was a tobacco man. Back and forth we went, and neither of us gave ground.

Then one day, out of nowhere, my father brought home a new tobacco hatchet. The rest, as they say, is history. The next year all our pull knives were put on the shelf, never to be used again.

I had to eat some serious crow with Hugh Green Jr. over those tobacco knives.

The sound of a tobacco stalk splitting over a spike is another sound of the tobacco harvest. If the spiker was skilled, that sound was followed by the hum of the spike as it rang like a muffled bell on the end of the tobacco stick.

I well remember the sound of tobacco tails sweeping the wagon or truck bed as my father swung loaded sticks of tobacco up into the barn and the sound of groans when an unusually heavy stick of tobacco was making its way up into the barn. And I remember the sound of yellow jackets buzzing around my head and tier poles creaking and the barn's tin roof popping from the heat of the sun.

All those familiar sounds take me back in time to days gone by. They are so closely tied to who I am. Sometimes when I recall them, my muscles ache.

CHAPTER 9

Tobacco Rows

● ● ●

I've spent some time traveling down rows of tobacco. In freshly plowed ground, I've struggled to keep my balance as I lugged a pressure sprayer filled with insecticide.

At other times I've walked, almost leisurely, with a hoe in my hands as I looked for stubborn weeds or grass. Then again, I've walked briskly down the rows topping tobacco, trying my best to keep up with the frantic pace set by my late father; he could take two rows at a time, topping with both hands, and never seem to slow down.

And I have cut and spiked tobacco in rows that seemed to grow longer by the minute. But my favorite recollections of tobacco rows are of the times when I was a small boy, probably ten years old. That was a time when a boy was expected to help but not to carry the full responsibility of an adult.

I remember the days before sucker control, the days before MH-30 and later Royal MH-30. Anyone familiar with tobacco knows that three suckers appear in the top of a tobacco plant soon after it is topped (when the terminal bud is removed). And when those three suckers are removed, the plant will "sucker" from top to bottom.

As growth inhibitors, the MH-30 family of sucker-control products brought sucker growth to a halt under proper conditions. But they also slowed the growth of the tobacco plant.

In the early days of sucker-control products, my father felt he got the most growth from his tobacco if we removed the initial top suckers after topping, before he applied MH-30. It meant more work, but it made for longer top leaves in the tobacco plants.

Needless to say, we pulled a lot of suckers in my growing-up years.

In the years prior to the arrival of MH-30, there were times when we were forced to pull suckers from top to bottom.

As a boy, I got the job of crawling down the row and pulling the bottom suckers. There is a world unto itself near the ground in a patch of mature tobacco. Hidden under a canopy of big, broad, drooping tobacco leaves, you could barely see the sky. Except during the hottest weather, the ground was cool and moist, made more so by suckers removed in earlier days. Sometimes, the suckers, fading from green to pale yellow, almost covered the ground. It made for a smell unique in the tobacco world.

And then there was the soil, deliciously soft and brown, giving up an occasional flint rock or arrowhead—soil that had a rich, clean smell about it. It was the kind of dirt that felt good in your hands as you rubbed off accumulated tobacco gum.

One year, after a prolonged dry spell, my father opted to "prime" one particular patch of tobacco. Down the rows my brothers and I went, removing the brown leaves from the bottom of each stalk of tobacco. As we worked along, we created piles of leaves at varying intervals. Later the leaves were picked up and moved to the tobacco barn for spreading out or stringing up. That year I was just the right size for the job. It was the only time I remember when working in tobacco was fun.

Of course, working in tall tobacco when you are a boy has another advantage. Because no one can see you, they don't know exactly where you are. So you can slip in a little "rest" now and then. My brothers contended I was real good at taking breaks in tall tobacco. Of course, I accused them of the same!

Those were good days. A boy came out of the tobacco patch at quitting time, with ground-in dirt on his knees and on the heels of his hands. Tired bodies make for the best sleep.

I learned many of life's lessons down those tobacco rows.

CHAPTER 10

Plowing Tobacco

● ● ●

Gone are the days when it was a common occurrence to see a man following a mule, or a pair of mules, or a workhorse through a tobacco patch or cornfield. Many a mile has been covered by a working man as he stumbled over newly turned-up earth while gripping worn plow handles. But no more. Those days, for the most part, are in the past.

I have often written that my father was a tobacco man. He approached growing tobacco as if it were an art. He seemed fascinated by every step in the process. I hardly think he considered it to be work.

Have you heard the saying "Love what you do, and you will never work a day in your life"? I believe that to be true. It was true of my father. From preparing the plant beds to stripping the last stalk, it was pure pleasure to him. He especially enjoyed plowing.

Through most of my formative years, I recall my father leaning over the steering wheel of a Farmall Super A tractor as he carefully studied the row passing slowly beneath him. At the first plowing each year, he took special pride in covering up all the newly emerging weeds and grass while not covering the tender yellow and green transplants.

Because of my father's skills with a plow, my brothers and I spent precious little time chopping tobacco. There may have been one or two wet springs when the grass "got ahead" of him, but for the most part, he kept the ground soft and the weeds and grass at bay with his plowing.

Prior to the Super A years, my father relied on "Ol' Charlie." I can't remember a time during my boyhood days when Ol' Charlie wasn't around. He was a big, black, rugged plow horse—I would guess, all of sixteen hands tall. Nothing seemed to bother him. I never saw Ol' Charlie get in a hurry. He had one speed—slow and steady. And he was smart.

In the days when tobacco plants (also called slips) were "pulled" (or drawn) from a plant bed, the young transplants sometimes encountered a rocky start. If the weather were unusually hot, the sun would sometimes burn some of the plants "back to the bud." Those tiny plants presented a special challenge at the first plowing, because they were easily covered up.

When plowing with Ol' Charlie under those circumstances, my father would watch for covered-up plants in the row he had just plowed. When he came "even" with a covered plant, he would call Ol' Charlie to a halt, reach over, and uncover the plant. After being stopped two or three times, Ol' Charlie would "get the hang of it." Then he would automatically stop every time my father came upon a covered plant. I think they call that "horse sense."

Plowing with a mule or horse was more complicated than plowing with a tractor. A tractor made one pass through per row. A horse or mule made two and a half passes. Each side of the row of tobacco was plowed, and then the plowman would "bust the middle" between the rows. Such plowing was accomplished with a three-point plow (sometimes called a "rastus"). As the tobacco grew larger, the plowman would resort to simply plowing the middle of each row. Sometimes that was done with a two-point plow or "double shovel."

In those days, a patch of tobacco might be plowed three or four times before it was "laid by." By "laid by," I mean the tobacco was dark green and growing and "lapping" in the row, making it impossible to go back through with tractor or horse or mule.

Today, tobacco is plowed as little as possible, and chemicals do most of the dirty work on weeds and grass. Why, I hear that in some parts, no-till tobacco is being tried. What is the world coming to?

Sadly, we don't hear much of horse collars and hames and trace chains and plowlines and single trees and clevises and plow handles anymore. Those days are gone. And, unfortunately, they took something with them.

The reason our fathers and grandfathers didn't lay awake at night and worry about their problems was they were too dog tired.

CHAPTER 11

Dropping Sticks

● ● ●

I found myself dropping sticks in a tobacco patch recently.

My son, Joseph, had professional cutters and spikers lined up, and he asked if I could help. I had some time on my hands, so I felt the least I could do was to pitch in. He quickly assigned me to dropping sticks.

Now to the uneducated, the term "dropping sticks" might sound a bit foreign. It is not as if you are walking through a tobacco patch and accidently let some sticks fall to the ground, like literally dropping a stick. Veterans of the tobacco patch, on the other hand, know that dropping sticks is a very important part of the tobacco-cutting (harvesting) process.

In years gone by, when cutting and spiking tobacco was a two-man operation, tobacco sticks were dropped on the ground between the two rows to be cut. As the cutter downed the two rows in front of him, he reached down, picked up a tobacco stick, and handed it to the spiker. Then he cut the next five or six stalks of tobacco and passed them back to be spiked.

As the plants were cut and spiked, another tobacco stick magically appeared in the row. Best I can recall, my brothers and I were taught to lay (or drop) the sticks end to end or let them overlap an inch or two. It was no small feat to tote an armload of tobacco sticks through big tobacco when dropping sticks that way. You kind of had to walk sideways.

In today's world, most tobacco is cut and piled by the cutters—five or six stalks to the pile. Later, when the tobacco has "fallen" (wilted), the same ones who cut the tobacco come back and spike it. Even though the process is different, tobacco sticks still have to be "dropped."

On the farm where I grew up, my father had a simple philosophy when it came to cutting tobacco: "Make it easy on the man who follows you." So we were taught "the art of dropping sticks."

It involved two unspoken maxims: (1) Don't make the spiker hunt for the stick. (2) If possible, have the stick land with the high end of the stick near the butt ends of the stalks in the pile.

This may sound a bit technical, but it was really very simple: "Pay attention to what you are doing."

I found early in my career that you have much more control over where and how a tobacco stick lands if you spin it as you let it go. That is especially true if you are dropping sticks on more than one row as you go through the tobacco patch. Anyway, I was afforded the chance to apply my skill last week.

As I left the house and started toward the tobacco path, my wife, Kathy's, last words were, "Now, don't you get out there and get too hot!" She sounded like she meant it. It was eighty-four degrees that afternoon. I was sixty-three years old at the time.

The first thing I realized was that a bundle of fifty tobacco sticks seemed much heavier than it did a few years back. I was huffing and puffing before I was finished transferring a few bundles from the wagon to the pickup truck.

By the time I arrived in the tobacco patch, I was sweating like a pig! And I was beginning to think I had bitten off more than I could chew. Not to be outdone, I threw myself into my work. Soon I was cracking open bundles and spinning tobacco sticks.

I was pleased to be reintroduced to the many personalities of tobacco sticks. I found two or three fashioned from a tree limb—dark in color, round, and straight. And there were still a few of the "split-out" variety—irregular in shape and one of a kind. There were skinny ones and heavy ones—some so big they felt like two by fours. And there were slick ones and splintery ones too. I was right there in tobacco stick-dropping heaven.

As the afternoon went on and the bundles of sticks seemed to get heavier, I noticed my legs seemed to be getting heavier, too. But at last, the job was done. And I was about done myself.

I climbed inside the pickup and headed to the house.

"Want to spike some?" Joseph called out as I drove by.

"Nope!" I answered.

The following Sunday, I was sharing my stick-dropping experience with a friend and telling of my sore muscles.

"Dropping sticks is what the women used to do when I was growing up," he said.

That was an un-Christian thing to say!

CHAPTER 12

Memories of My Dad

● ● ●

I HAVE OFTEN SAID I am one of those fortunate sons who can say my father was the best man I have ever known. They just didn't come any better than Frank T. McCall. I could write a book about him, and someday I just might.

He was the oldest of nine children born to DT and Amy Manning McCall. And all his life he commanded (not to be confused with "demanded") the respect of his younger brothers and sisters. Everyone liked to be around my dad.

He was unassuming, almost bashful, and a man of few words—and "honest as the day is long."

My dad loved the land. Farming was his life. He especially loved growing tobacco. He approached each new crop with the same determination and enthusiasm. It was art to him. He carefully studied the nuances of the cultivation of the soil and all of nature's complexities that related to each crop. He used to constantly refining his craft, and he knew what he was doing. In all the years he farmed, he never had a crop failure.

Frank T. McCall never met an internal-combustion engine he didn't like. He had "the knack" for anything mechanical. I thought it bordered on genius. If an engine went bad, he was undaunted. He would tear down an engine in a heartbeat.

In thinking of my dad and his farming years, I find him and an A-Model John Deere tractor almost inseparable. Somewhere in the early life of the tractor, he removed the electrical starter. To start the tractor, he either "rolled it off" or started it by hand.

He knew that tractor like the back of his hand. And he could back a four-wheeled hay wagon anywhere he decided—even down the narrow hallway of a tobacco barn. It was no small feat.

In the life of that old John Deere, my dad overhauled the engine twice. He literally knew it "inside and out." I can see him now, perched high in the tractor seat as that old John Deere rolled along, spitting and hissing.

My mother, my brothers, my sister, and I always helped in getting the tobacco crop out. But once the growing was under way, my dad took over.

In the early years, he plowed behind an old black horse named "Old Charlie." In later years, he used his trusty Farmall Super A. We were called in to help with topping, sucking, cutting, and hauling. But for the most part, my dad enjoyed being alone. He spent a lot of time alone with his crops.

My dad insisted, "Oil is the life of an engine." And when he was working with machinery, he always carried a gun...a grease gun. Every piece of equipment on his farm was well oiled and got an extra shot or two of grease. He had big, strong mechanic's hands, with black under his fingernails.

I recall this with fondness: if the sermon got slow in church on Sunday, he would take out his pocketknife and clean the black dirt out from under each of his fingernails.

My dad's clothes always smelled of diesel. My mother explained that was why he was never bothered by chiggers, ticks, or three-leaf poison oak.

He wore long underwear nine months out of the year. He switched from boxers to long johns in September and didn't switch back to boxers until late May.

He carried a big, four-blade pocketknife. One blade he kept "sharp as a briar," and he used it for castration only. But his favorite little tool was a small pair of Xcelite pliers that would fit into the palm of your hand. He called them his "nippers."

In most situations, he preferred those pliers to his pocketknife.

Although he never said so, I think being elected to serve as a deacon in his church was one of my father's life-crowning achievements. He had a simple testimony, and he lived it every day.

Shortly after my father's death, I was one day thinking of him and prayerfully considering the bountiful blessings our family has enjoyed.

Our father referred to it as "our many blessings" when he prayed in public. Over many years our family members, for the most part, have been strangers to hospital corridors. We are, indeed, a family blessed.

As I pondered all this, deep within my spirit came the answer, "Your father was a praying man." And I realized that when many of those times my father was alone with his crops, he was also alone with his God.

And to this very day, we continue to reap the benefits of his life and his prayers.

CHAPTER 13

Boyhood Memories of Dew Roy Neal

• • •

It was with no small degree of sadness that I read in The Carthage Courier of the passing of Mr. Dew Roy Neal a few years back.

I was visiting my second cousin, Jerry Holbrook, in New Middleton, Tennessee, when I first met Dew Roy Neal. Both Dew Roy and I were in our tenth year that summer. There are a number of things I took away from that three-day visit.

One night I got sick on peach ice cream. My grandfather, Herod Brim, always said there was nothing sick like being sick on peach ice cream. He was right. I have never been so sick at my stomach—not before then and not since.

On the second day of my visit, we spent the day setting tobacco on the Ralph "Pappy" Holbrook farm. Ralph Holbrook, who married my mother's first cousin, Ruth (we called her "Aunt Ruthie"), was sharp-witted and quick with a smile. He wore a dress shirt and a necktie when he worked in his general store in downtown New Middleton, when he went to the milk barn, and when he worked in the tobacco patch.

Best as I can remember, Dew Roy Neal's family must have been growing tobacco on "shares" with the Holbrooks. There were a bunch of new faces present. Dew Roy's father was there and, of course, Dew Roy.

We spent the morning pulling (drawing) tobacco plants (slips) out of a plant bed. Pappy Holbrook made sure there was a lot of joking and kidding going on. By the time the morning was over, he had convinced me that a mullein weed, found occasionally in the plant bed, was a special kind of hybrid tobacco plant grown for seed. Everyone was in on the joke but me.

It was also on this summer visit that I was first introduced to a "job-setter" or "a dry-land peg." Recently I saw one at the Log Cabin Pancake House in Gatlinburg. I would try to describe a job-setter to my readers, but you have either both seen and used one or you haven't.

It is hard to describe. Let me just say its use is labor intensive. It seems there were a dozen of us in that tobacco patch that afternoon. Lots of good-natured kidding and name-calling was the order of the day. Since I was a "guest," I got the best end of it. By the close of the day, I sensed Dew Roy had just about had enough of me.

The next day, they say he came looking for me to whip me, but I had already left for home. But Dew Roy would have his day. It would come three years later.

I don't remember much about my basketball-playing days as a seventh grader. I do have vivid memories of my eighth-grade year. I made the first team for the "little boys" or junior boys at Carthage Elementary School. We were all less than five foot six in height. The "starters" were William Denney, Harold Poindexter, Jimmy Hackett, Hugh Green Jr., and me.

Our main competition in the county that year was New Middleton.

Those New Middleton boys could play some ball! I don't remember all their names. There were the Winfree brothers, William and Wesley; the Baker boys; the Wills boys and a host of others; and, of course, Dew Roy Neal. They were coached by Crump Paris, the man for whom the local park is named.

We beat New Middleton twice during the regular season and, eventually, came to face them in the finals of the county tournament that year. In the minds of my teammates and me, it was a given that we would win again. It was a whale of a game.

With the game winding down and time running out, New Middleton pulled ahead by a score of 38–35. With less than a minute to go, the ball came to me at the head of the foul circle. I heaved a desperation shot from there that banked in the goal: 38–37.

New Middleton took the ball in bounds, and our coach, Joe Smith, called for us to foul. We did. A New Middleton player went to the line to shoot foul shots. He missed.

With the final seconds ticking away, we raced to the other end of the basketball court in hopes of winning the game.

As I write this column, I can clearly see in my mind's eye Harold "Digger" Poindexter (at one time or another we called all those Poindexter boys "Digger") twisting and turning, trying desperately to get off a last shot with two or three of those New Middleton boys draped all over him. The referees chose not to call a foul, as time ran out. New Middleton had won!

It was a hard pill to swallow. But I shall never forget how happy those New Middleton boys were, especially Dew Roy Neal.

In the ensuing forty-plus years, I only ran into Dew Roy a couple of times. The passing of time has brought me to this conclusion: I'm glad those New Middleton boys won that game. I wish I had taken the opportunity to tell Dew Roy how I felt about it.

Every boy should experience what the late Jim McKay of ABC's Wide World of Sports called "the thrill of victory." I'm glad Dew Roy Neal had his moment.

CHAPTER 14

A Good Humor

● ● ●

My first venture into the working world was as a short-order cook at the G&R Dairy Chef at the age of thirteen. That was 1964. The original floor plan of the G&R remains largely unchanged today under the name of Brenda's Restaurant in Carthage, Tennessee.

I made many friends as a waiter at the G&R, many of whom I considered to be "old" at the time. Most were probably in their fifties. When you are thirteen, fifty seems old. Many were regulars on the weekend. Others would stop in several times a week for a cup of coffee. I particularly remember Bill and Florence Carter, Mr. Walter Beasley, and Mr. Bob Mixon.

Mr. Mixon was one of my very favorites. He had an easy way about him and an infectious grin. I was always glad to see him drop in. I called him "Mr. Bob."

Mr. Bob was one of the founders of Mixon-Nollner Oil Company, located in South Carthage. As a teenager, I perceived him to be a fine individual, as well as a successful businessman. For those reasons, I made an effort to keep up with him as the years passed. It was always a pleasure to run into Mr. Bob. There are a few people from whom you choose to learn.

One day, when Mr. Bob was well into his seventies (or maybe even his eighties!), I called him on the phone and asked if I could "come and see him." He very graciously granted my request. A few days later we met at his house on a sunny, summer's afternoon.

Mr. Bob lived in a big, white-framed house located on the hill just east of Monoville on Highway 80. Today, it still sits majestically up on the right-hand side of the road about a quarter mile from downtown Monoville.

We sat in his backyard that day under giant shade trees and talked away the afternoon. When the time came for me to leave, he said, "Before you go, I've got something to show you. Come with me."

He strolled leisurely in the direction of his garden, which lay just east of the backyard. I followed along. When we were in full view of his garden, he stopped to give me time to take a good look. I could hardly believe the sight that met my eyes.

Now, I had seen gladiolas before. But my experience was limited to a few yellows and whites, usually in flower arrangements in church or in funeral arrangements. But that which was growing in Mr. Bob's garden that day almost took my breath away.

Two full rows of gladiolas stretched out before us. There seemed to be every color under the sun—bold, vivid, vibrant colors: reds and yellows and oranges and whites, varying shades of pink, and even dark purple. I stood in stunned silence for a moment, wide-eyed, with my mouth dropped open.

My reaction pleased Mr. Bob to no end. He beamed with pride.

"Now, that'll put you in a good 'umor, won't it?" he said with a sly grin.

"It surely will, Mr. Bob," I answered as I shook my head in wonder.

Many years have flown by since that summer day, but I have not forgotten either the sight of those flowers or the weight of Mr. Bob's words.

Those of Mr. Bob Mixon's generation used the word "humor" in an interesting and powerful way. Pronouncing the word with a silent "h," they spoke of one being in a "good 'umor." You might call it being in a good "mood" or a healthy frame of mind.

I can think of a lot of things that put me in a good 'umor. My granddaughters have unique smiles. Whenever they smile their smiles, I cannot help but laugh out loud. They always put me in a good 'umor.

A big plate full of fresh-cooked vegetables, right out of the garden, puts me in a good 'umor. I've been in a good 'umor a lot here lately.

Inspiring music can put me in a good 'umor.

Apostle Paul wrote that it is important to think on such things that are good, honest, pure, and just.

I have found that if you do not focus on the good, you have a tendency to dwell on the bad.

As I was thinking of things that can put one in a good 'umor, the words of an old hymn began to scroll across my mind:

> I have a Savior who loves me, I know.
> He's guiding and guarding wherever I go.
> He walks beside me along the bright way.
> His love grows sweeter each day.

CHAPTER 15

Gravel Roads

● ● ●

THERE ARE THREE GRAVEL ROADS that stand out in my memories.

One stretched a quarter mile south from the front of our house to Highway 70. Today, a section of that gravel road is called Watervale Lane. It links up with today's County House Circle to complete the stretch of road to Highway 70.

Back in the day, County House Circle was called the Old County House Road. My great-uncle's store—Dewey Manning's General Store—stood at the intersection of the Old County House Road and Highway 70.

Dewey Manning's Store was a center of activity in the community of Watervale. For that reason, the members of the Frank McCall family made many a trip down that gravel road.

I well remember one of the first times I walked the length of that road alone. My mother had sent me on an errand to the store.

It was before I started to school, and I wore a sunsuit, so I could not have been much older than five. In those days a little boy was perfectly safe on a deserted country road. It was a time when everybody in a community knew everybody else.

I too remember the first few times I crossed the stock gap that marked the boundary of our farm as I walked that road. I can still recall the feel of those rough oak boards beneath my bare feet as I stepped from one beam to another, careful not to fall between the timbers.

My brothers, my sister, and I walked that gravel road to catch the school bus at the storefront in our younger days. We walked it in the cool of the morning and in the heat of the afternoon in the spring and early fall, and we walked it when we had to run to stay warm in the dead of winter.

The Old County House Road holds some special memories for me.

We used that road to move farm machinery when we farmed my grandfather D. T. McCall's land on McCall Lane. My father chose to use a stretch of Old Highway 70 and the Old County House Road to avoid the main highway. I learned a lot about gravel roads on the Old County House Road.

I learned you couldn't lay down on an empty hay wagon when you were going down a gravel road. If you did, when you hit a bump, that wagon would knock the breath right out of you. I've had it happen more than once.

Sitting on the wagon bed was almost as bad. It was better to stand, but it was hard to keep your feet.

I remember the first time my father let me take a tractor back home on the Old Country House Road. I remember how I felt: proud, excited, and half scared. I learned some things about brakes, speed, and loose gravel on the Old County House Road.

The third gravel road I remember well is the road into the Brim Hollow. I know that road like the back of my hand. I traveled it most often with my grandfather, Brim, in his 1951 GMC pickup truck. The funny thing is, in thinking back, I can smell the inside of that old truck as I write these lines.

I had never walked that gravel road until the spring of my eleventh year.

On occasion, I would visit my grandparents in the middle of the school week. That involved taking the school bus to Riddleton. My grandfather would be waiting for me when I got off the bus at Leonard Carter's store. But one particular afternoon when I arrived in Riddleton, my grandfather was not there to meet me.

I had money to buy the Nehi grape soda and Hershey bar, which he would have purchased for me, and sat down on the store porch to wait for him. He didn't show up. Something was wrong. I continued to wait.

With the afternoon beginning to slip away, I made the decision to start the two-mile walk into the Brim Hollow. I wanted to make it before dark.

Along the first mile, I encountered all the fears a young boy can conjure up on a journey fraught with uncertainty. What had gone wrong?

Would Pa Rube be all right? Would I run into a rattlesnake? Or a mad dog? A bobcat? A ghost?

I had made it over the most challenging hill and through the first creek bed, when I faced a long shady lane in which deep shadows were beginning to fall.

I noticed my pace had quickened along with the stepped-up beating of my heart. That's when I heard a most beautiful sound. It was the chug-chug-chug of Big Jim Yancy's old army Jeep. Big Jim was a neighbor and friend to my grandfather.

He brought his Jeep to a stop beside me.

"What you doing out here, Jack?" he asked in a booming voice.

I told him of my predicament.

"Well, get in here," he said with a broad smile. "I'll take you the rest of the way."

My grandfather had had a "spell" with his heart and had taken to the bed for a few days.

The next morning my granny, Lena, got me up early, and we walked those two miles of gravel road together. I caught the school bus right on time.

You have probably heard of a "godsend." That's what Big Jim Yancy was for me late one evening on a gravel road.

CHAPTER 16

Pope's Hill

● ● ●

AFTER MY FATHER DIED IN 2003, I drove to Carthage almost every Saturday morning to visit my mother.

Highway 25 from Hartsville to Carthage is a pleasant, scenic drive to which I always looked forward. The closing of the Cordell Hull Bridge, however, posed a dilemma of inconvenience for me. Taking the bypass around Carthage had me doubling back to US Highway 70 and on to Watervale.

Coming from Hartsville, I found it saved time and distance to cross the Cumberland River in Trousdale County and travel through Providence and Hiawassee. Consequently, I intersected Highway 70 just east of Flat Rock and just west of Rome (Tennessee, not Italy).

Driving that stretch of road from Hiawassee to Watervale for the years up until my mother's death filled me with nostalgia. I recalled many people, places, and events. The drive also reintroduced me to Pope's Hill.

As you travel west, Watervale Lane, which leads directly north to the old homeplace where I grew up, intersects Highway 70 exactly 3.1 miles from the south end of the Cordell Hull Bridge. Approximately one mile further west sits Pope's Hill. It is the highest and the steepest hill that Highway 70 crosses between Carthage and Lebanon.

My mother told me years ago how Pope's Hill got its name. As the story goes, two brothers, Adkins and Phillip Pope, were traveling down the Cumberland River in search of a place to settle.

Adkins Pope left the river east of the hill near Watervale and set up camp, where he eventually built a cabin. Phillip chose to travel further west. So the brothers parted company, not knowing if they would ever see each other again.

Two years later, Adkins Pope found himself hunting game on the top of the hill.

Looking westward he saw smoke rising in the distance. With musket in hand, he decided to investigate the situation. What he found at the source of the smoke was a cabin and his brother, Phillip. They had lived within two miles of each other for the past two years, unaware of each other's whereabouts. The hill is rightfully named for the Pope brothers: Pope's Hill.

This story was confirmed by Donna Pope Dennis, a direct descendent of Phillip Pope. She also provided me with the names of the Pope brothers.

Traveling from the west, two things stand out for me on the western slope of Pope's Hill. On the right-hand side of the road, my late friend and fellow class of 1969 member Benny Watts once grew an outstanding garden each year. I mean, he did it right. It did my heart good just to watch Ben's gardens growing over the years.

On the other side of the road is an open field, where a sawmill once operated.

J. C. Owen owned that mill. I'll bet if you dug deep enough into the ground, you would find sawdust.

As you cross the hill from the west, a frame house stands on the left. It used to be white. It is beige now with a green top. My great-aunt, Bessie McKinney, once lived and raised a family there. She was my grandfather D. T. McCall's sister.

I have all kinds of McKinney cousins, many to the first, second, and third power. Dr. Roger McKinney, who practices good medicine in Lebanon, is a second or third, or maybe fourth, cousin. His father, Dave, grew up on Pope's Hill.

As you travel from the east and crest the top of Pope's Hill, if you look down and to your left, you will see a white frame house with a green tin roof.

For most of the last century, Mr. Charlie Midgett lived there. He and his wife, Miss Mary, raised a family of fine children in that house. Mr. Charlie was instrumental in starting a Sunday-school program at Plunkett's Creek Missionary Baptist Church.

Over three decades after his death, that Sunday school is still going strong. The good that some men do lives after them.

My mother told me a man named William Leonidus Marion Lucas Stiflukanus Sky George Rufus Thompson once lived on or near Pope's Hill.

"They called him Bill," she said.

My lifelong friend and Smith County historian, the late Frank Gibbs, informed me that Mr. Thompson was named after twelve of his uncles. I may have left out a name or two.

CHAPTER 17

The Smell of Skunks

• • •

I suppose, of all the smells of country living, the smell of skunks is the most odoriferous. (I was about to write "odorous," but I discovered the word "odoriferous" when I looked it up in *Webster's Dictionary*.)

Of course, the smell of rotten eggs should be right up there with skunks and hogs, but the smell of rotten eggs just doesn't have the staying power of the other two.

I have been hit with a rotten egg in the middle of a corncob battle, I have been sprayed in the face by a skunk, and I have worked around hogs most of my life, so I know of what I am writing.

Several years ago there was a rabies epidemic among the Middle Tennessee skunk population. You might remember that summer. Skunks seemed to be everywhere. I would guess, over the period of a week or two, I saw at least a dozen or more dead skunks on the highways and country roads in various places. The entire skunk population was very active. It was most unusual.

I have a longtime friend named Mack Jordon, who lives in Chapel Hill, Tennessee. We talk on the phone pretty regularly.

In the latter part of that same summer, the subject of skunks came up in one of our conversations. He informed me that one of his neighbors had killed over twenty skunks in a very short period of time. It seems as though skunks were acting strangely all over the Middle Tennessee area.

Mack retired from working for the Tennessee Farm Bureau Federation several years ago. But after his retirement, he continued to attend the Annual Tennessee Farm Bureau Convention held each year in Nashville. In early December following the previously mentioned summer, he was again in Nashville, attending the annual convention.

At the convention, Mack noticed that his friends and acquaintances were giving him funny looks whenever they approached him to exchange pleasantries. It became so obvious that he asked an old friend if there was something wrong with him. The friend, who was a true friend, said, "Yes, Mack, you smell like a skunk!"

That set into motion a thorough investigation. Over the next few days, Mack found out that not only his clothes but also everything in his house smelled like a skunk.

Come to find out, several weeks earlier, one of those skunks his neighbor shot had crawled up under Mack's house and died. Slowly, but surely, and ever so subtly, that skunk smell had infiltrated his entire house. Anything that was permeable had to go.

All the clothes of his family had to be sent to the dry cleaners for special cleaning; it was the same for all the drapes. All the carpet had to be replaced. All the cloth furniture had to be removed and required special fumigation. His wife even took advantage of the opportunity and changed out the kitchen cabinets.

Fortunately for Mack, his homeowner's insurance covered the cost of all the damages (except for the kitchen cabinets). Mack came away from the experience with a new respect for skunk power.

When I was a boy, I was sprayed directly in the face by a baby skunk. Don't let the word "baby" fool you. Those little buggers come into this world loaded. At point-blank range, skunk spray does not smell like skunk. It is pure ammonia. It is way beyond nauseating. And it is blinding to the eyes. My hair turned green.

On the day that skunk sprayed me, I was wearing an orange short-sleeved shirt handed down from my brother Tom. Of course, those were the days when you didn't throw anything away. After washing me in a Purex bleach bath, my mother ran that orange shirt through the washing machine a time or two.

Both my younger brothers later wore that shirt. But my mother testified that every time she ironed that shirt in the ensuing years, she got a whiff of skunk smell.

Now that's staying power.

CHAPTER 18

The Rifleman

● ● ●

I can well remember the black-and-white television. I can also remember the Sunday evening our entire family loaded up in our pickup truck and went over to a neighbor's house to get our first look at television in living color. It was a few years before my father brought home our first color set.

My brothers and I grew up watching three channels. Later on, if you had a special antenna, you could pick up Channel 17. Then, still later, Channel 30 came along. But for the most part, it was three channels.

I'm proud to say that my wife, Kathy, and I raised our three boys on those five basic channels. Not until our youngest graduated from high school in 2002 did I break down and install DIRECTV. That's not to say I didn't endure plenty of grief over the years for my unwillingness to go multichannel via satellite. But I held my ground as long as I could.

Suddenly we had over two hundred channels. And I promise you, sometimes in the years that followed, I have found myself sitting there after going through the channel menu and thinking, "There's not a thing on tonight that's worth watching!"

Then, a while back, my youngest son, Joseph, saved the day when he suggested I add the Outdoor Channel and the Western Channel. Happy days are here again!

Not too long ago, I was having a conversation with a young man who finished college last fall.

"What's your favorite Western?" I asked.

He gave me a blank look and replied, "What's a Western?"

I didn't know what to say. *What's a Western?* Why, no wonder the world is going to Hades in a hand basket! What's a Western, my eye!

Recently I was reintroduced to the classic Western series *The Rifleman*. Now there's a real Western for you. Starring Chuck Connors as Lucas McCain, *The Rifleman* showcases all the drama and excitement of the Old West. Lucas is (what would be called today) a single parent raising his son, Mark. Played by Johnny Crawford, Mark is a good boy. I know he is a good boy because his main lines in the series are "Yes, sir, Pa!" "Why, no, sir, Pa!" "I'm sorry, Pa" and "Sure, Pa!"

When Lucas tells Mark to do something, he does it. Mark is a good boy.

I know of a bunch of childhood actors whose lives turned out to be train wrecks. But I'll bet Johnny Crawford grew up to be a fine man. He's got that look in his eyes.

Lucas has this specially modified rifle that fires automatically when he pumps its lever. A ring in the lever affords him great freedom in wielding his firearm. Lucas McCain can pump a dozen rounds through that Winchester faster than a cat can lick his whiskers. He doesn't have to call on his rifle in every episode, but he rarely goes anywhere without it.

Lucas and Mark seem to spend a lot of time in town. That's where most of the action takes place. The other two main characters are the sheriff, Micah, Lucas's trusted friend and "Miss" Millie, who operates the general store.

In most Westerns, the general-store operator is a wimpy little man who wears glasses—not so on *The Rifleman*. Miss Millie is a sweet little thing and, as Mark says, "Purdy, too!" I think Lucas is a little sweet on Miss Millie. But if he is, their courtship is limited to an occasional invitation out to the McCain Ranch for supper. Lucas is much too focused on raising his son to have much time for courtin'.

According to Mark, Lucas is a great cook, especially when it comes to baking apple pie. (However, on the show, Lucas spends precious little time in the kitchen.)

In every episode of *The Rifleman*, an important life lesson is brought to light. The show usually ends with Lucas pointing out that lesson to his son, Mark.

I found I could sit down in front of my television precisely twenty-two minutes before bedtime, and if I fast-forwarded through the commercials, I could watch an entire episode of *The Rifleman* and still get to bed on time.

And the lessons Lucas teaches his son leaves me with the best feelings. I go off to bed with good thoughts in my head.

Good, wholesome entertainment is hard to come by these days—the kind that takes you back to the thrilling days of yesteryear, when doing the right thing and living right meant something.

It makes me a little homesick just thinking about it.

CHAPTER 19

A Visit with an Old Friend

• • •

SOME FEW WEEKS BACK, I decided to go visit an old friend. So I packed up some gear and headed for the Brim Hollow. I took two chainsaws, a twelve-gauge shotgun, and my favorite little ax; but most importantly, I took my time. You can't be in a hurry when you spend time with a friend.

When I go there, it is like turning back the clock fifty years. Sometimes when I'm there, I can be caught talking to myself. Or maybe I'm just talking to the memories.

Regardless, I always feel a strange but familiar closeness to my late grandfather, Will Herod Brim, as I walk the Brim Hollow.

When I first arrive, I'll say something like, "Hello, old friend. I'm sorry I've been away so long." Places filled with fond memories have a wonderful forgiving quality about them. I have always sensed a response of "welcome back."

On the day of my return, the air had a wonderful feel about it. It was cold but not too cold. It was a good day for cutting up a big limb that the wind had twisted out of a cedar tree. I went right to work.

After I had cut it into firewood, I decided to split up some kindling. There is no kindling quite like dried cedar. The first stroke of my ax yielded a sound I had not heard in years. Dried cedar makes a unique sound when being split. I stopped to savor the sound as I smelled the cedar.

After the wood was loaded onto my truck, I laid my shotgun on my shoulder and moseyed on up the hollow. I was tempted to look at my watch, but I refused. Reflection is becoming a lost art. I wanted this visit to be unhurried.

At an old springhouse, I lingered to observe how the rocks had been laid so carefully, and I wondered how long it took to build it. Then I studied a network of rock fences brought low by time.

Soon I found myself high in the head of the hollow, rounding a windy ridge. A tobacco patch once lay there, a patch we affectionately called "the mountain." It was now grown up in trees. I was surprised by the size of some. It was hard to believe tobacco once grew there.

I observed how, in years past, a strong wind had cut across the ridge, leaving a half dozen big oak trees downed in its path. One now lay across the tobacco patch. Its trunk, black from decay, provided a stark contrast from the bright-green moss that grew on its topside.

As I walked across the field, I looked down to see the sharp-featured faces of rocks that had pushed themselves up through the decaying leaves. And I remembered how those rocks nicked and cut our bare feet when we pegged tobacco in this unforgiving ground.

I had circled the west side of the hollow when I arrived in a place we call Squirrel Tail Hollow. There I noticed the ground was heavy with undisturbed walnuts and hickory nuts. (We used to call them "hickernuts.")

I wondered if the squirrel supply was short this season, or if the hollow had received an abundance of rainfall the year before. I looked up to see one of the fattest squirrels I have ever seen. He was so fat but flat across his back. When he saw me, he stood still; I think he was too fat and lazy to run. I laughed at his indifference.

Soon I had made a full circle of the hollow and stood in front of the old feed barn. I stopped and peered inside. A ladder led into the barn loft.

I have climbed that ladder a thousand times. In the crib of that barn, I have cranked a corn sheller until my arms ached. I hesitated for a moment to picture dry shucks, yellow corn, and red corncobs.

On my way back to the truck, I stopped by the old homeplace. It was beginning to fall down. I looked through the window into the bedroom, where I once slept in a featherbed under a mountain of quilts. It is the room where my grandmother's quilting frame hung from the corners in summertime. I thought of all the quilts she had made.

As I left the hollow that day, I felt a sense of wholeness that I had not experienced in a while. I had been reminded of who I am and where I came from, of the people and of the things I have loved, and of the fabric of which I am made.

As I shut the gate behind me, I whispered, "Good-bye, old friend. I promise not to be away so long next time."

NOTE

NOTE

NOTE

Made in the USA
Charleston, SC
07 September 2016